To

From

101 QUICK TIPS
TO MAKE YOUR HOME
LOOK
SenseSational

Books by Terry Willits

101 Quick Tips to Make Your Home
Feel SenseSational

101 Quick Tips to Make Your Home
Look SenseSational

101 Quick Tips to Make Your Home
Smell SenseSational

101 Quick Tips to Make Your Home
Sound SenseSational

101 Quick Tips to Make Your Home
Taste SenseSational

Creating a SenseSational Home

If you are interested in having Terry Willits speak to your
church, organization, or special event, please contact:

InterAct Speaker's Bureau
8012 Brooks Chapel Road, Suite 243
Brentwood, Tennessee 37027
Telephone (800) 370-9932
Fax (615) 370-9939

101 QUICK TIPS
TO MAKE YOUR HOME

LOOK
*Sense*Sational

TERRY WILLITS

ZondervanPublishingHouse
Grand Rapids, Michigan

A Division of HarperCollins*Publishers*

101 Quick Tips to Make Your Home Look SenseSational
Copyright © 1996 by Terry Willits

Requests for information should be addressed to:

ZondervanPublishingHouse
Grand Rapids, Michigan 49530

Library of Congress Cataloging-in-Publication Data

Willits, Terry, 1959–
  101 quick tips to make your home look SenseSational / Terry Willits.
    p.   cm.
  ISBN: 0-310-20224-8 (hardcover)
  1. House furnishings.   2. Interior decoration.   3. Christian life.   I. Title.
TX311.W536   1996
645—dc20   96-13330
                                                                              CIP

This edition printed on acid-free paper and meets the American National Standards
Institute Z39.48 standard.

Edited by Rachel Boers
Interior Illustrations by Edsel Arnold
Interior design by Sherri Hoffman

Printed in the United States of America

96 97 98 99 00 01 02 /❖ QF/ 10 9 8 7 6 5 4 3 2 1

— ⚜ —

He has made everything

beautiful in its time.

Ecclesiastes 3:11

Introduction

― ⚜ ―

$\mathcal{G}$od has given us eyes as windows to his world. Much of how we interpret life comes from what we see. And because we spend more time in our homes than perhaps anywhere else on earth, making them pleasing to our eyes can greatly affect our outlook on life.

Beauty is all around us. Every glimpse gives us a chance to notice something lovely. But since we are able to take in so much of the world at one time, it is easy to get distracted and fail to focus on the magnificent beauty right before us.

May the following tips inspire you to open your eyes to the beauty around you and bring a few fresh touches to your corner of the world — your home. Keep in mind, sometimes the smallest bits of beauty mean the most. God bless your home as you bring beauty to it!

terry.

101 QUICK TIPS
TO MAKE YOUR HOME
LOOK
SenseSational

Wake up to the beauty around you.

Open your eyes to the beautiful world God has created and discover what delights you. Notice the rainbow of colors and vast array of shapes and sizes and textures in nature. Let God's awesome creation inspire you to create a home that is pleasing to your eyes.

2

Begin a "my favorite things" box.

$\mathcal{U}$se a decorative shoe box or hatbox to collect favorite items like trims, fabric swatches, ribbons, paper napkins, stationery, or other colorful memorabilia. This box will help you discover the most appealing color scheme for your home.

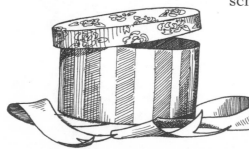

Color your world.

*G*od, the Master Artist, has painted beautiful colors on his outdoor canvas. Which colors please you the most? Color shapes every sight and influences every emotion. Surround your private world in the rainbow of your choice. You are the artist. Your home is your canvas.

4

Start a "dream" file.

*C*ollect pictures from your favorite home magazines for creative inspiration and future reference. File your clippings by room in an accordion file or a pretty notebook with clear vinyl sheet protectors. As patterns emerge in  what catches your eye, you will begin to discover your decorating style.

Be on the lookout.

$\mathcal{O}$bservation is one of the best ways to train your eyes and learn what pleases you most. Tour model homes in newly developed neighborhoods. Wander through furniture showrooms. Visit decorator showhouses. Go on home tours. Take your camera and a notebook, documenting anything you love.

6

Make home where your heart is.

*Y*our home should reflect the personalities, passions, and priorities of those who live there. On a piece of paper, list the personalities, passions, and priorities of each member of your family. Ask God to help you convey these as you decorate your home.

Make your front door friendly.

*Y*our front door is an outsider's first impression of your home. A pot of flowers, a wreath, a welcome sign, a fresh coat of paint or varnish, shiny hardware, clean light fixtures, a brass kick plate, or a pretty doormat all say welcome!

8

Shine on!

For a long-lasting shine, wax freshly polished or new brass hardware (lacquered or unlacquered) with a quality lotion-type automobile wax. Let dry and buff with a soft cloth.

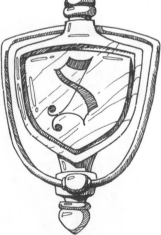

Glitter with glass.

A clean window allows you to fully enjoy the beauty beyond it. Clean your home's windows inside and out at least once a year, using warm water and vinegar as a cleaning solution. For sparkling appeal from the street, remove the screens on your front windows.

10

Get rid of grungy garages.

*I*f your garage is the first place you see when you arrive home, try to keep it orderly. Stain a concrete garage floor a dark color to hide oil and dirt. (Stain won't peel or chip like paint.) Paint garage walls with a durable, semigloss paint so that you can wipe away any marks.

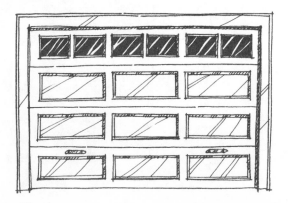

Clean it up by clearing it out!

$\mathcal{Y}$ou cannot have beauty without order. Disorder distracts the eye. Clearing the clutter in your home will bring beauty to the forefront. Take advantage of organizational books and stores that feature organizational tools. Focus on one small area at a time. If organization is not your bag, ask an organized friend to help you get started.

12

Clean as you go.

*A*rrive at a practical compromise for cleanliness and sanity. If things are orderly and lovely to look at, a little dust or dirt won't be as distracting.

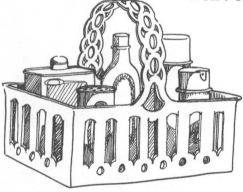

13

Begin with something beautiful.

*I*f you are wondering where to start to make a room pleasing to the eye, begin with what you have and love. Then work your way up, starting with the floor, furniture, walls, windows, and, finally, accessories.

14

Let it flow, let it flow, let it flow.

*F*ind one beautiful fabric or wallpaper for your main living area that has a pattern and colors that you love. Use this as the color palette for your entire home. Other rooms may only use one or two colors from this palette, but it will provide a smooth transition between rooms.

15

Try it before you buy it.

*B*efore buying yards of fabric or rolls of wallpaper, put the pattern on trial. Tape a large sample of your selection to a wall in the room in which you plan to use it. By looking at it and living with it for several days or weeks, you

will be better able to
determine if the pat-
tern is right for you,
possibly avoiding a
costly mistake.

16

Welcome with color.

*P*lace a favorite piece of artwork, a hand-hooked rug, or a cozy wing chair in your entrance to introduce your color palette and to hint at the collage of colors yet to come.

Unite with white.

To allow a smooth transition between rooms, paint all trim on windows, doors, and moldings the same neutral color. Consider using a high- or semigloss, white oil-base paint. (White works well with all colors, and oil-base paint is the most durable for woodwork in your home.)

18

Paint it pretty.

*P*aint is the least expensive way to transform a room — but before you break out the roller, buy a quart of the color you have selected and sample it on a piece of poster board or foam-core, looking at it in the daytime and night-time. Use an eggshell or satin finish on walls and semigloss or high-gloss finish on trim. For an added touch, paint the inside of a closet to match the color of the walls.

Keep your head up!

For heightened interest, stir one cup of the color paint you use on your walls into a gallon of white ceiling paint. When painted, the ceiling will slightly reflect the wall color. For an airy touch, paint a ceiling sky blue with clouds. For instant intimacy, paint the ceiling to match the walls.

20

Have fun with faux.

$\mathscr{E}$xperiment with different painting techniques to give a custom look. Sponge paint, marbleize, or stencil walls, furniture, or floors. A little paint and elbow grease can go a long way toward turning a room from mediocre to marvelous.

Let there be light!

*L*ight was the first element created by God; it is energizing, welcoming, and helps us to see the beauty around us. Use three-way bulbs in lamps to alter a room's atmosphere. Place a spotlight on the floor behind a plant or folding screen for indirect light and dramatic shadows.

Hang picture lights to warm the colors of paintings. Use track or recessed lighting to high-light specific areas.

22

Seek the unique.

When selecting lamps, consider wiring an object into a lamp such as a brass or silver candlestick, a porcelain teapot, or a ceramic vase. A lamp shop can wire and mount almost any object onto a base. Select a pretty shade and decorative finial for a lovely custom lamp at a reasonable price.

Redress a lamp.

*U*pdate an old lamp with a new shade. Customize your shade by covering it in fabric or banding it with trim or fringe. (Many lamp stores offer this service.) Top off your lamp shade with a decorative finial.

24

Tie on a tassel.

*D*ecorative tassels add a touch of color and class. Try hanging one from a lamp, a candlestick holder, a ceiling fan, a piece of artwork, or a key in a chest or secretary.

25

Create instant impact.

$\mathcal{D}$ecorate your living room around a focal point such as a fireplace, a cherished piece of furniture, or a window with a garden view. If possible, have your sofa face the focal point or have two love seats flank it.

26

Keep it looking good.

*C*onsider applying stain-resistant finishes to
light-colored upholstered furniture or to
carpet or rugs in major traffic areas. Although
these finishes will need to be reapplied after
cleaning, they will help reduce soil and keep
things pleasing to the eye.

Move it!

*R*earrange furniture for a new look, making sure your favorite pieces are placed in positions for you to enjoy. Move furniture into groupings to create conversational areas or to take advantage of views. For coziness, draw furniture in a few feet from the walls. For interest, place a sofa on a diagonal.

28

Keep it cozy.

*I*n the winter, place a big basket of seasoned logs beside your fireplace. Summerize your fireplace with a decorative painted screen or a large basket of flowers or plants.

Entertain elegantly.

*U*se an old linen press or armoire to house television and stereo equipment. If the doors will remain open, remove them and rehang them in reverse so that the decorative sides will show.

30

Create a homey hearth.

*W*arm up your mantle with a favorite collection, a beautiful piece of artwork, a decorative mirror, or a welcoming wreath.

31

Warm your home with wood.

$\mathcal{D}$etermine which woods please you the most and provide the look you want. For an eclectic feel, tastefully mix a few finishes. For a rich look and luster, refinish a dull piece of old furniture and add new hardware.

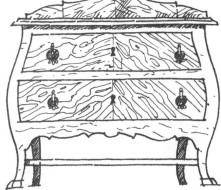

32

Create a clever coffee table.

For a unique, one-of-a-kind coffee table, find an old dining table with character and cut down the legs. Or find an interesting base and top it with a piece of heavy glass. Sturdy trunks work well too, as well as provide extra storage space to help keep clutter to a minimum.

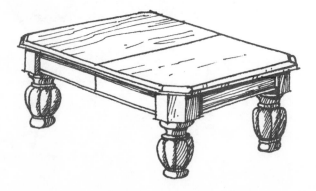

Store memories by the bowlful.

*P*ut a big bowl or basket on your coffee table and fill it with family photos that haven't yet been filed into albums. Not only is it a fun and easy accessory, it's a great conversation starter or memory jogger.

34

Freshen up with flowers.

*B*ring God's bountiful beauty into your home with a colorful bouquet of flowers. Make it a ritual when you go to the grocery store or farmer's market to pick up a bunch. Select those that appeal to you and go with your color scheme. They will lift your spirits as they please your eyes.

Cluster a collection.

$\mathcal{M}$ake it a fun hobby to collect a particular type of object that appeals to you — candlesticks, porcelain, pottery, bunnies, brass, vases, teapots. For visual impact, display the collection together.

36

Beautify your bookshelves.

*A*dorn your bookshelves with beautiful books. Place all hardback books together, removing jackets and pulling spines flush to the edge of the shelf. Stack large books horizontally on shelves or a coffee table. Place a pretty book on a plate stand, letting its cover face forward.

Accent it.

*F*or a splash of color, paint a contrasting or accent color behind your bookshelves. Before you do, though, test the color on a piece of foamcore and slip it behind the bookshelf to make sure you like it.

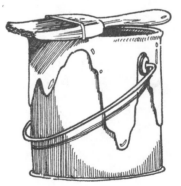

38

Create one-of-a-kind bookshelves.

For a clean, dramatic look, fill your bookshelves with something other than books: all baskets, all colored glass, all wooden artifacts, all hats.

Browse through beautiful books.

*C*ollect beautiful books with photographs of places you have visited or things that you love, marking your favorite pictures with fabric ribbon. Display the books on a coffee table as a lovely reminder of your past or your passions. When you have a brief moment, sit and browse through your books and get lost in their beauty.

40

Charm with chairs.

*I*ntrigue the eye with the unpredictable. Unify two different style dining room or kitchen chairs by upholstering them in the same fabric. Or, let wing chairs stand in place of the usual end chairs. Vary matching chairs by recovering or slipcovering seats with different fabrics.

41

Break it up!

A tasteful mixture of furniture makes any room more interesting and pleasing to the eye. Breaking up a matching set of furniture lets each piece's beauty stand on its own. Try using a bedroom dresser for a buffet service in the dining room or using a bedside chest for an end table.

42

Go on a treasure hunt.

$\mathcal{S}$earch flea markets, junk shops, antique shops, and estate sales for beautiful bargains. It doesn't cost anything to look! If something catches your eye the minute you see it, there's a good chance it reflects your decorating style.

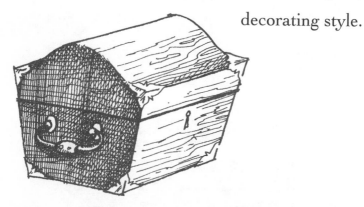

Make the ordinary extraordinary.

*M*ix dinnerware. Collect pretty dishes and glasses that work well together. Combine your grandmother's china with goblets from a flea market. Mixing fine things with less expensive ones gives both priceless charm.

44

Create casual elegance.

When decorating your dining table, be creative and mix finishes. Combine flower-filled terra cotta pots or wicker baskets with crystal or silver accessories such as candlesticks. The eclectic combination will intrigue the eye.

Bring God's beauty indoors.

*P*lants are an inexpensive way to give life, color, and warmth to any room. A hearty plant like a philodendron, pothos, or peace plant only needs to be watered once a week and fertilized with plant food once a month. Use spray-on leaf polish to keep plant leaves shiny and healthy.

46

Let your chandelier take center stage.

$\mathscr{E}$nhance your chandelier by topping its bulbs with miniature shades, which are available in many colors, sizes, and styles. For a custom look, cover the shades with fabric, paper, or paint, and finish them off with trim. Soften the look of a chandelier's chain link by covering it with a shirred sleeve of fabric.

Switch it.

Replace ordinary electrical switch plates in visible places with more decorative ones. Buy quality brass switch plates, paint wood switch plates to match trim, or cover switch plates with wallpaper used in the room.

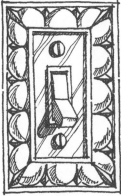

48

Cluster candleholders.

*U*nify a group of candleholders by using only one color for all candles. Although you can put together all sizes and shapes, stick to one or two materials: wood, brass, crystal, or

silverplate. If a candle is too narrow for the holder, wrap the candle's base with a small fabric doily or a rubberband to add bulk and make it fit. Use elegant eighteen-inch candles for special occasions.

49

Dim it!

*D*im the lights and light a candle when you sit down to dinner, even when dining alone. This gracious gesture takes just seconds, but sets the tone for your meal and your mind-set.

50

Add a special sparkle.

*F*or a flickering focal point in any room,

place a large pillar candle on an Oriental

wood base and surround it with a

hurricane globe.

51

Make magic with mirrors.

A mirror can visually expand a room and lighten and brighten a space with its reflection. Have a beveled glass mirror cut for an old, large frame. Or, for instant impact, collect a variety of smaller, interesting mirrors from flea markets and assemble them into a collage on a wall.

52

Update kitchen cabinets.

 ew hinges and knobs can bring life to old kitchen cabinets. Try ceramic knobs that color coordinate with your kitchen accessories. Display tableware by replacing a few cabinet doors with glass doors. Or simply leave doors off cabinets, paint the interior cabinet walls, and have open shelving.

Make appliances appealing.

*I*deally, appliances should visually coordinate with the kitchen decor. If they don't, epoxy paint can be used to change their color. Change the front of a dishwasher by slipping an inexpensive piece of laminate in its place. For an extra touch, have a pretty design handpainted on the laminate.

54

Beautify your burners.

*I*f you have an electric stove top, enhance your burners with enameled cooktop covers. Available in several colors, they save clean-up chores and create extra workspace while hiding unattractive burners.

Clear it off!

*I*nstead of hanging everything on your refrigerator doors, place an attractive bulletin board in an unobtrusive but convenient spot to hold information or homemade artwork. If you do use your refrigerator for display, edit it often, and make it as pleasant as possible. Use acrylic magnetic frames for refrigerator photos.

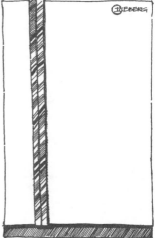

56

Keep countertops clutter-free.

*D*isplay only utensils and portable appliances that are functional and beautiful; store all others. If it's time for a new appliance, consider an under-the-counter model to give your kitchen a cleaner look and increase work space.

Fascinate with food displays.

*F*ind creative and beautiful ways to display food items in the kitchen. Store flour, sugar, coffee, and tea in lovely canisters. Buy a pretty cookie jar to store cookies. Put dried, colorful pastas in oversize glass containers. Pour spices into small apothecary jars and arrange on a wood rack. Fill colored or clear glass bottles with flavored oils and vinegars.

58

Show it off.

*H*ang a simple shelf across a kitchen doorway or window. Load it up with attractive kitchen accessories that you love, but use less frequently. This will keep fragile items in view, but not in the way. Pot racks are a great way to display beautiful, but necessary cookware or baskets.

Display pretty plates.

*F*or a touch of charm, place decorative plates anywhere and everywhere. Prop them on plate stands. Hang them with either a wire hanger that slips onto the back of the plate or on a decorative rack that holds several plates at a time.

60

Buy a beautiful bed.

$\mathcal{S}$ave your pennies and buy a bed that suits your style — you'll enjoy it for years. Place your bed in a spot where you have the greatest view while lying in it. For a cozy look, try angling the bed from a corner. For a romantic look, raise any bed frame by placing it on sturdy blocks.

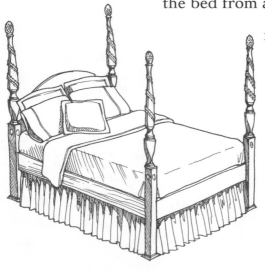

61

Mix and match fabrics.

$\mathcal{T}$ake the guesswork out of decorating with ready-made collections of coordinated fabrics, wall coverings, and bed linens. To mix your own, look for remnant fabrics. Try mixing plaids, checks, stripes, polka dots, geometrics, or textured solids with a large pattern.

62

Double up.

*M*aximize your decorating possibilities using a duvet cover with a different fabric on each side. Flip it when soiled or simply for a new look. Give your dust ruffle a deluxe, designer touch by using one long and one short one. Or, if they are the same size, pull up on the top one and pin it to the box spring to create the same look.

63

Add pizzazz with pillows.

$\mathcal{U}$se pillows to personalize any piece of furniture from a handsome chair to a hand-me-down sofa. When piling pillows on a bed, use a variety of different shapes, sizes, colors, and fabrics for visual interest. For a custom look, tie a ready-made pillow with a decorative tassel or fabric bow.

64

Keep your sheets sweet.

$\mathcal{U}$se pretty, decorative sheets to beautify your home. They're well-priced, extra wide, and often have coordinating, ready-made pillows and comforters to adorn your bedroom. Or, for a pleasing table decor, turn a pretty sheet into a tablecloth and matching napkins.

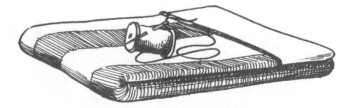

Make it up.

*T*ry to establish a habit of making the bed as you leave it in the morning, and teach your family to do the same. Certainly, there are carefree times that call for an unmade bed; but more often than not, the simple task of bed-making sets the tone for the day and helps a bedroom look its best.

66

Put on a skirt.

A skirted table is an economical way to add color and coziness to any room while providing out-of-sight, but close-at-hand storage. Embellish a table skirt with cording, fringe, banding, or a ruffle. Top it off with a lace or fabric overlay and a round piece of glass.

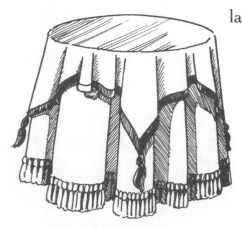

Express your heart with artwork.

*A*llow your passions to be expressed with your artwork. Sentimental treasures like christening gowns, heirloom lace, children's artwork, menus from special restaurants, or baseball caps can be framed for life-long memories.

68

Warm up a wall.

$\mathcal{H}$ang colorful quilts, tapestries, or hook rugs on large walls, using a piece of wood and Velcro strips. Each can bring a touch of handmade charm to any wall in your home.

Hang up your heritage.

$\mathcal{M}$ake your heritage a focus in your home by filling a hallway or stairway wall with framed photographs of family. Collect and frame black-and-white photographs of ancestors to keep track of the family tree, marking relatives' names in permanent, black ink on the back of each frame.

70

Keep it at eye level.

When selecting artwork, balance the visual weight, color, and scale of the artwork with that of nearby furnishings. When installing artwork, hang at eye level. (In a hallway, eye level would be when standing; in most other rooms, eye level would be when seated.)

Angle your art.

For a friendly, casual look, prop a piece of artwork atop a mantle or chest rather than hanging it. Or mount a high chair rail with a groove to rest artwork on. When leaning several pieces together, vary height and sizes. Angling art keeps decorating flexible and fresh looking.

72

Frame your favorite faces.

*R*emember, relationships are the most important part of life. Collect pretty frames and fill them with the faces of those you love. Groups of photos look best with frames made, at least partially, from the same material to visually unite them.

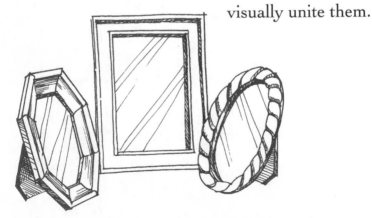

Decorate down under.

When accessorizing a sofa table, don't forget to decorate beneath it too. Use large plants, stacks of big books, baskets, old leather luggage, or anything unique that will lend warmth and charm.

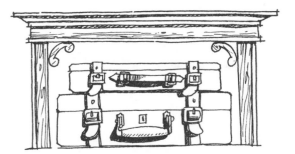

74

Have fun with a fan!

*J*azz up a ceiling fan by painting the blades to match walls or a colored ceiling. Or paint each blade a different color, handpaint them, or cover them with wallpaper. When feeling conservative, flip fan blades over to original finish.

Put it on a pedestal.

$\mathcal{D}$raw the eye to a special artifact or trophy by placing it on a pedestal. Raise objects such as a small lamp, clock, or picture frame to new heights on pedestals of stacked books or wooden boxes.

76

Decorate with baskets.

*B*askets of all sizes, shapes, and colors can be used to decorate and organize the home. Adorn the tops of kitchen cabinets or the refrigerator with baskets. Fill them with magazines and place them in bathrooms. Use lidded baskets beside your kitchen phone and bed.

Make the most of your trash.

Natural, wicker trash cans are attractive and reasonably priced. Surprise the eyes by placing a pretty paper doily at the bottom of each. Try using a large, lidded wicker hamper for a kitchen trash can. It holds lots and looks warm and friendly.

78

Button up!

Use covered or decorative buttons to enhance your pillows, window treatments, upholstered furniture, picture frames, or lamp shades. They're inexpensive, yet add an unexpected, unique touch that delights the eye when discovered.

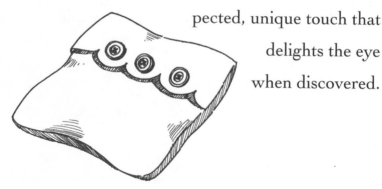

79

Create an "instant" antique.

*T*ransform a plain plaster or concrete sculpture into a beautiful accent piece by brushing or sponging on a wood stain finish or brown shoe polish. This trick will also turn homely, hardback books into rare and beautiful treasures.

80

Be unpredictable.

*A*dd a touch of whimsy or humor when decorating a room. Display a painting by a relative, a pair of cowboy boots, an old bicycle wheel — anything that makes you stop and smile.

81

Delight your desk.

*F*ind attractive, creative ways to display your necessary desk accessories. Consider using a small decorative vase to store pens or a silver toast rack to hold bills, letters, invitations, and correspondence.

82

Think about it.

*K*eep a daily thought flip calendar by your kitchen or bathroom sink to inspire you at a glance and fill your mind with good things.

83

Top your table tastefully.

When accessorizing the top of any table, think of it as an empty canvas on which you can apply colors, shapes, and textures. Put low objects towards the front and tall ones toward the back.

84

Hide and seek.

To keep rooms fresh and pleasing to the eye, rearrange accessories frequently. By putting some away temporarily, and bringing others out, you will appreciate their beauty more.

Discover hidden treasures.

*P*ull out those treasured wedding gifts tucked away in cabinets. Use a lovely silver dish for potpourri or a crystal bowl for a pretty candle. Don't overlook the family attic — you may uncover a hidden heirloom that can add a piece of family history to your home.

86

Contrast it.

*L*ike an outline to artwork, contrasting colors can please the eye and add punch to a room. Try colorful pillows on a neutral sofa or dark lamp shades in a room with light walls. Use contrast cording or banding on upholstery, window treatments, or pillows.

Make your windows wonderful.

indow treatments should provide privacy and enhance a room without blocking outside light, air, and beauty. Keep your window treatments consistent with your decorating style.

88

Simplify, simplify.

*D*on't overdo when decorating. The eye can only enjoy so much at one time. Edit what you see. What you leave out is as important as what you leave in. A simple bowl filled with one kind of fruit cannot be surpassed for beauty.

Pair it.

$\mathcal{B}$eautiful objects arranged in simple symmetry draw the eye to them. When possible, buy two of the same accessory. This gives you the flexibility to show them side by side or use them in two different areas.

90

Brighten chores with friendly faces.

*H*ang an attractive bulletin board filled
with photographs of family and friends above
your washing machine. Their faces will
brighten your day as you do laundry, and
will remind you to pray for them.

91

Paint a piece to beauty.

$\mathcal{R}$evive an old piece of furniture by painting it. Bring life and charm to a room by painting an outdated kitchen table and chairs. Hand-paint a "ho-hum" chest with a happy design on its drawer fronts. Spruce up an old wicker rocker with a coat of pretty paint.

92

Light up the night.

Turn on your front porch lights at night for a
friendly glow. Set prominent lamps on timers to
welcome family home and keep thieves away.
Use pretty night-lights in all your bathrooms
to light the way for children,
guests, and even yourself!

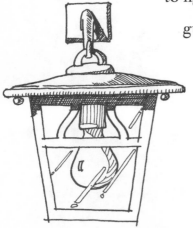

Keep it out
of sight.

$\mathcal{S}$tore all personal beauty products and
appliances in bathroom cabinets. If space
is limited, add a touch of charm
and storage to the room with a
small chest or cabinet.

94

Behold bottles
of beauty.

A pretty wicker shelf in your bathroom
is the perfect place to display decorative
glass bottles of mouthwash, lotions, and
bubble bath.

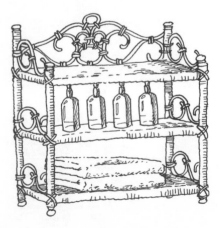

95

Use natural objects to decorate.

A seashell by the bathroom sink can hold soap or jewelry while you wash. A knotted branch can be used as a rod to drape a casual window treatment. Bamboo shoots hung horizontally can hold bouquets of dried flowers and make wonderful wall arrangements.

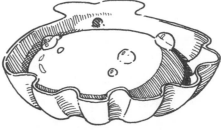

96

Spruce up the shower.

*E*nhance your bathroom with a pretty shower curtain. Buy a decorative one, or make one from a flat sheet, tablecloth, or fabric. Try adding color to a simple, white shower curtain by tying it to a curtain rod with grosgrain or other fabric ribbon bows that coordinate with bathroom decor.

Make a splash with color.

*B*ring color into your bathroom with pretty towels and throw rugs that coordinate with the room's decor. Don't stash color in a closet: hang towels on wall pegs or roll them up in a large basket beside the tub.

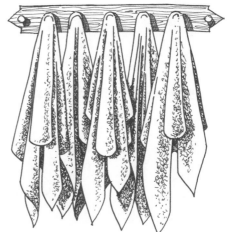

98

Cover it up.

To hide damaged or wallpapered walls or ceilings or to simply add visual interest and texture, put sand or stucco mixture in paint. Try upholstering a wall with fabric shirred on curtain rods or by stapling batting to the wall, then

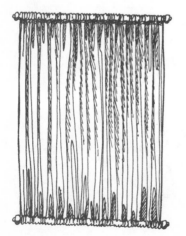

stretching and stapling fabric over the batting and finishing off the stapled edges with cording or trim.

Paint your paneling.

Painted paneling lends clean, crisp, cottage charm to any room and makes a beautiful backdrop for colorful accessories. It gives a textural interest that smooth walls can't achieve. Paint existing paneling or add paneling before painting a room.

100

Take care of yourself.

*E*ach morning when you get up, get dressed, brush your hair, and apply some makeup. When you look good, you feel better. When you feel better, it affects your home's atmosphere.

101

Create lasting beauty.

*I*nner beauty far outlives any of the fabrics or furnishings that fill our homes. Make it a priority to spend time in God's Word. As you communicate with him, he will inspire you with the most creative ways to bring beauty into your home. Remember, he is the One who makes everything beautiful in its time.

More from Terry Willits . . .

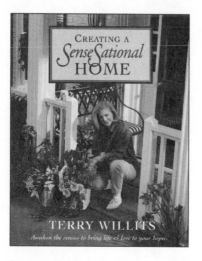

Creating a SenseSational Home is the complete guide to discover how awakening the five senses of sight, smell, taste, touch, and sound can create an atmosphere of love and cheer. From warmly-lit entrances that welcome family and friends to comfortable, homey interiors that invite them to stay and unwind . . . from fragrant bouquets to the tranquil ticking of a clock . . . *Creating a SenseSational Home* shows you simple and affordable ways to turn your home into a relaxing, inviting, and refreshing environment.

ISBN 0-310-20223-X
$19.99

ZondervanPublishingHouse
Grand Rapids, Michigan
http://www.zondervan.com

America Online
AOL Keyword:zon

A Division of HarperCollins*Publishers*